Join in
Jump on...

Join in – Jump on!

Scripture Union
207-209 Queensway, Bletchley, Milton Keynes, MK2 2EB, UK

Writers: Margaret Cluley, Zoë Crutchley, Sue Dunn, Muriel Griffith, Veronica Parnell,
  Christine Wright
Editor: Marjory Francis
Design: Chris Gander Design Associates   Illustration: Branwen Thomas

ISBN 185999 3222
© Scripture Union 2000

Printed and bound in the UK by Ebenezer Baylis & Son Ltd, The Trinity Press,
Worcester and London

To help you

This book will help you to read stories about Jesus and his friends in the Bible. The Bible is made up of lots of books. Here are the ones you will be reading from:

Matthew Mark Luke John Acts

They are all in the New Testament. See if you can find them here and colour them in:

Matthew | Mark | Luke | John | Acts | Romans | 1 Corinthians | 2 Corinthians | Galatians | Ephesians | Philippians | Colossians | 1 Thessalonians | 2 Thessalonians | 1 Timothy | 2 Timothy | Titus | Philemon | Hebrews | James | 1 Peter | 2 Peter | 1 John | 2 John | 3 John | Jude | Revelation

In this book find out about:

Exciting times *Days 1 to 4*
Puzzling times *Days 5 to 11*
Sad times *Days 12 to 17*
Happy times *Days 18 to 29*
Amazing times *Days 30 to 35*

Plus:
Lots of Extra pages
The joke and puzzle page!

Note to parents:
In this book your child will be reading about the first Easter, beginning with the story of Palm Sunday. It will be difficult to always read the "right" story on the "right" day, but if you wish to fit reading **Join in – Jump on!** around Easter itself, it may help you to know that Day 16 is Good Friday and Day 18 the first story of Easter Day. A suggestion for making Easter cards can be found between Days 20 and 21.

How to use this book

There are Bible activities in this book to keep you busy for 35 days. You will find the Easter story, from Palm Sunday to Pentecost, which you can read in the Bible. And there are lots of ideas to help you get to know God better. Each day you will find

- something to read
- a puzzle or questions to answer
- something to look up in the Bible
- a prayer idea

Sometimes there are Extra ideas too!

Here are some ideas as you **Join in – Jump on!**:

- It's best to read it every day if you can, but it doesn't matter if you miss days sometimes. Just carry on from where you got up to.
- It's OK to **Join in – Jump on!** on your own, or you might like someone to help you.
- Most days you will just need a Bible and a pencil to **Join in – Jump on!**
- It's best to save the Extra pages for when you have lots of time. You will need to collect other things to use for these.
- Try to find somewhere quiet to read your Bible and **Join in – Jump on!**

So make sure you have a Bible and a pencil, and jump on to **Join in - Jump on!** now.

Exciting times

One day Jesus was with his friends. He told two of them to go a village where they would see a donkey. Jesus said, "Untie the donkey and bring it here."

 Read the story in **Mark chapter 11, verses 1 to 6.**

Lord

needs

What were Jesus' friends to tell people if they were asked why they were untying the donkey? Find the missing words on the page. You will need to write each one twice.

"You must say _ _ _   _ _ _ _   _ _ _ _ _
_ _."

The friends untied the donkey. Some people asked, "What are you doing?" The friends said,

"_ _ _   _ _ _ _   _ _ _ _ _   _ _", and

the people let them go.

it

Which rope do the friends need to untie to take the donkey?

 *prayer time*

Exciting times

I am one of the friends who Jesus sent to get the donkey. We took the donkey to Jesus. The donkey's fur was rough, so we put our coats on its back for Jesus to sit on. As we walked along the road, people joined us. Some threw their coats on the ground like a carpet.

What did other people do?

the story in **Mark chapter, 11 verses 7 to 8** to find out.

Lord Jesus, all the people shouted praises to you when you rode on a donkey into Jerusalem. Help me to praise you every day.

The people cut branches off the trees. How many branches can you find hidden in the picture? (The answer is upside down at the bottom of the page.)

I can find ☐ branches.

Lots of people joined in and there was a procession. It was very exciting.

Answer: There are 6 branches

Exciting times

Jesus was riding the donkey into Jerusalem.

Read Mark chapter 11, verses 9 to 10 to find out what the people shouted.

prayer time

If you had been in the procession, what would you have shouted in praise to Jesus? Draw yourself here and write what you would have shouted.

Say the words you have written as a prayer. You can shout them out if you want to.

Extra!

Colour t

Shaker
Put coloured pasta shapes inside a clear plastic drinks bottle or a plastic pot. Attach coloured paper streamers.

Rainstick
Cover a cardboard tube with coloured paper. Put rice inside and tape paper over the ends.

picture

praise Jesus with!

Trumpet
Cover a cardboard tube and a plastic cup with foil. Tape the cup to the tube and attach coloured paper streamers.

Harps
Cover a shoebox in coloured paper and wrap elastic bands around it. Attach coloured paper streamers.

Exciting times

Jesus and his disciples went to the temple, the place in Jerusalem where people worshipped God. They saw people doing their shopping there. Jesus wanted the temple to be a special place.

Mark chapter 11, verse 15.

What did Jesus do? He turned over the

What did Jesus say? Find out in **Mark chapter 11, verse 17.** "You have made God's house a place for..."

Colour the shapes by the things that Jesus wants us to do when we go to church.

say a prayer ◯

dance ▢

hurt someone ✚

play "Hide and Seek" ☆

fight ▽

read the Bible ◇

sing songs to praise him ♡

Think about a special way that you can praise and say "thank you" to Jesus. Lord Jesus, I want to praise you by

Puzzling times

Auntie Meg is coming to visit. Tick the things that Kate might do to show that she loves her.

Make a welcome card ☐

Arrange some flowers in her room ☐

Lock the door to keep her out ☐

Go off with friends and leave her alone ☐

Give her a hug and a kiss ☐

What else might Kate do?

In the quiet little village of Bethany, Jesus and his friends were invited to dinner at Simon's house. While they were eating, a woman brought in a beautiful jar of perfume. It had cost a lot of money. She treasured it more than anything else. Usually she used just a drop for herself at very special times, like weddings and parties.

LOOk up

Mark **chapter 14, verse 3** to find out what she did with it.

She poured it on Jesus'

e d h a

Lord Jesus, please help me to show I love you by the things I do.

The woman gave her most precious thing to Jesus because she loved him so much.

☑

Puzzling times

When the other guests saw and smelt what the woman had done, they were angry.

What a waste!

It could have been sold

The money could have been given to poor people

You foolish woman!

What a silly thing to do!

But read **Mark chapter 14, verse 6** and find out what Jesus thought of what she did.

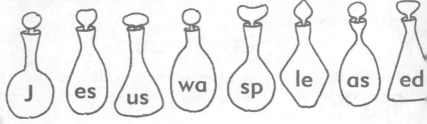

J es us wa sp le as ed

a prayer

Write the letters on the perfume jars in the spaces below.

— — — — — — — — — — — —

Lord Jesus, please help me to learn to do what pleases you.

Do you think Jesus is pleased with what you have done today?

Puzzling times

It was time for the great Passover Festival! Families and friends celebrated it each year with a special supper party. They remembered how God had wonderfully saved their people from slavery in Egypt many, many years before.

Jesus' friends asked where they were to get their party ready. Jesus gave instructions to Peter and John. You can read them in **Mark chapter 14, verses 13 to 15**.

Find out: **Where** Jesus told them to **go**.
             Who he told them to **meet**.
             Where he told them to **follow**.
             What he told them to **say**.

Peter and John had to listen carefully to the instructions and then follow them. Can you find the person Jesus told them to meet in the crowd?

Please God, help me to listen carefully to what I am told to do at home and school.

Puzzling times

Circle the things that you would get ready for a party.

Peter is telling us what he and John had to get ready.

We followed Jesus' instructions carefully and found an upstairs room. There was a table with room for us all to sit round. It was just right. We started to get the festival supper ready. We roasted the lamb, washed the herbs, bought the flat bread and made sure there was enough wine. We had to work quickly because Jesus and the others would arrive as soon as it got dark.

prayer time

You can read about this in **Mark chapter 14, verse 16**.

Are you getting ready for something special at home or school? Get ready now to talk to Jesus. Shut your eyes and keep quiet for a moment. Talk to Jesus about the things you will be doing later today or tomorrow. Ask him to help you do them well.

Puzzling times

The food was ready, all cooked with care,
When our friends, with Jesus, climbed the stair.
They were dusty and tired and feeling the heat,
But nobody offered to wash their feet.
"Such a nasty job", so they all thought,
"Is only for servants, and not our sort."

But somebody did the dirty job. Read **John chapter 13, verses 4 and 5** to find out who it was.

_ _ _ _ _ _ did the job nobody else wanted to do.

Think: Could you be more help at home?
Join up the dots in the right order to find out who needs all these things doing.

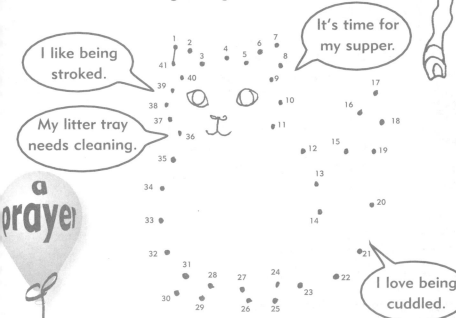

I like being stroked.

It's time for my supper.

My litter tray needs cleaning.

a prayer

I love being cuddled.

Help me, Jesus, to be more like you and cheerfully do my share of the dirty and boring jobs.

Which would you choose to do?

Puzzling times

Peter couldn't bear to think that his important leader was doing a job like washing his feet for him.

Jesus, you're never going to wash my feet!

If I don't wash your feet you can't be one of my friends.

All right, but wash all of me.

I don't need to do all that, Peter. You had a bath this morning.

prayer time

Find this story in **John chapter 13, verses 6 to 10.** Jesus did the dirty job because he loved his friends. He wanted them to be comfortable and enjoy their supper.

Think of the people who do things to make you more comfortable. Draw one of them.

Put some names into this prayer.

Thank you, God, for _____

and _____ who work hard

to make me comfortable.

Puzzling times

Jesus and his friends were eating their Passover supper. They ate the lamb, bread and herbs. They remembered how good God had been to their people in the past, and praised him for it. But then Jesus did and said something quite new.

 what it was in **Mark chapter 14, verses 22 and 23.** This was the way they were to remember what Jesus did for them.

Look at Mark chapter 14 and fill in the spaces.
Simon's house was at B _ _ _ _ _ _ (**verse 3**).
Perfume was poured on Jesus' h _ _ _ (**verse 3**).
The friends looked for a man carrying a jar of w_ _ _ _ (**verse 13**).
Jesus arrived for supper in the e _ _ _ _ _ _ (**verse 17**).

Jesus b _ _ _ _ the bread (**verse 22**).
He gave it to the d _ _ _ _ _ _ _ _ (**verse 22**).

Fit your answers into the grid. The shaded squares will spell what Jesus gave to God.

Sad times

After they had eaten supper, Jesus led his friends to a garden. It was night-time and very dark. When they arrived, Jesus said, "Sit here while I pray." But he asked three of his friends to be close to him while he prayed.

Jesus was very sad. He knew that he would soon have to leave his friends and that he was going to die. He prayed that he would please his Father God.

Who were the three friends Jesus took with him?

 Mark chapter 14, verse 33 and write their names here. The last letters are written already.

_ _ _ _ r

_ _ _ _ s

_ _ _ n

Draw the three friends with Jesus in the garden. Remember it was night-time!

a prayer

Lord Jesus, you know what it's like to be sad. Be close to me and be my friend when I am sad. Amen.

Sad times

Suddenly Jesus and his friends heard noise and saw flaming torches! It had been quiet in the garden, but now lots of other people were there. Some had swords and wooden clubs. They had come to arrest Jesus and take him away. It was very unfair because Jesus had not done anything wrong. Worst of all, one of his own friends had shown them where Jesus was. Find out who it was by looking in **Mark chapter 14, verse 45.**

Find the letters of his name around the page and write them here.

Look for him in the picture below. (He is not holding anything!)

Can you remember when something unfair happened to you or one of your friends? Say "thank you" to Jesus that he understands what it's like when unfair things happen.

Sad times

Peter followed the crowd who had arrested Jesus. He was very angry and upset because he loved Jesus and didn't want anyone to hurt him. He watched as the crowd took Jesus into a big house and waited outside to see what would happen. Then a servant girl spotted Peter. "You are one of Jesus' friends," she said.

What did Peter say? Find out by reading **Matthew chapter 26, verse 70**. Then colour in the right answer below.

I only met Jesus once.

I am Jesus' best friend.

a prayer

I don't know what you're talking about.

I am sorry, Jesus, that I sometimes do wrong things and let you down. Thank you for forgiving me. Thank you that I can still be your friend.

Peter had let Jesus down. Later, Jesus forgave him. He still wanted Peter to be his friend.

Sad times

Some of the words in this story are wrong and are written in bigger letters. But they all rhyme with a special word (the same word every time). Try to guess the special word.

The people who arrested Jesus said, "He is pretending to be a **wing**. We must take him to Pilate and tell him to put Jesus to death."

Pilate asked Jesus, "Are you a **ring**?" Jesus replied, "It is you who have said I am a **sting**."

So Pilate told the people who arrested Jesus, "I don't think that Jesus has done anything wrong."

But they wanted to get rid of Jesus, so they said, "He is telling all the people that he is a **thing** and we are afraid that the people will get angry and start making trouble for us and for you."

Now read **Luke chapter 23, verse 3** to see whether you guessed the word correctly. Write it here:

Say your own prayer, thanking Jesus for being your friend and your _ _ _ _ (the special word!).

Sad times

This is the saddest story of all. But it has a very happy ending which we will hear about soon.

Soldiers took Jesus to a place outside the city. There they killed him by putting him on a cross. On the cross they hung a notice which said, "This is Jesus, the king of the Jews."

Some of his friends watched Jesus die. They loved Jesus and were very sad about what was happening to him.

Find the story about Jesus dying in **Matthew chapter 27, verses 35 to 38.**

Jesus was not the only person who died on a cross that day. Can you draw the right number of crosses in the picture below?

a prayer

Lord Jesus, I am sad that you had to die, but I am glad that, very soon, something wonderful happened. Whether I am sad or happy, stay close to me and be my friend.

Extra!

This is a special prayer to say when something has gone wrong. This is how to say it:

First, spell the name **J e s u s**, touching your thumb when you say the letter **J** and your next finger when you say **e** and so on. Then do it again, this time saying one line of this prayer as you touch each finger.

Jesus, I'm glad you're with me,
especially when I'm
Sorry
Upset or
Sad

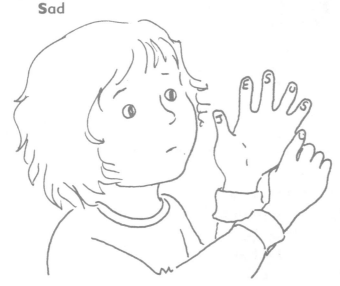

Sad times

Jesus had died on the cross. His friends thought they would never see him again. In the evening on the same day, three of his friends found ways of showing that they loved him.

A rich man called Joseph went to Pilate. He said, "Let me have Jesus' body." Then he took it, wrapped it carefully in a sheet and laid it gently in a tomb (like a cave). Two women, both called Mary, sat outside the tomb, watching what Joseph was doing. They wanted to know where Jesus was buried.

Look at **Matthew chapter 27, verse 60** to find out how Joseph closed the tomb. Draw it in the right place in this sad picture and, if you like, draw some flowers in the garden to brighten it up.

prayer time

Thank God for the good friends that Jesus had, and then for your friends, especially those who help you when you are sad.

Happy times

The women were very sad. On Friday they had watched their best friend Jesus die on the cross. Early on Sunday morning they went to the tomb to put some sweet-smelling spices on Jesus' body. When they got there, they had a shock. The big stone had been rolled away from the entrance of the tomb! When they looked inside, they had an even bigger shock.

Luke chapter 24, verses 3 and 4 to find out what they saw – and even more important, what they did not see!

Draw what the women saw at the tomb.

Write here what was missing:

o d y b   e u s J s

the _ _ _ _ of _ _ _ _ _

Dear Father God, sometimes I don't understand what is going on. Help me to trust you.

Happy times

Mary Magdalene loved Jesus very much. He had been her special friend and now he was dead. She was so sad that she could not stop crying. She didn't want to leave the tomb. Do you remember that there were two angels there? They spoke to her.

Why are you crying?

LOOk up

John chapter 20, verse 13 to see what Mary replied. Colour the shape with the correct answer.

prayer time

They have taken away

the stone

the body of Jesus

the grave clothes

Say "thank you" to Jesus for always being with you. If you know someone who is feeling sad at the moment, ask Jesus to be with them in a special way.

She didn't know that soon she would have a wonderful surprise. Draw Mary's face.

Happy times

Mary was at the tomb, still crying. She saw a man standing nearby. She thought he was the gardener. He asked her who she was looking for.

Tell me where Jesus' body is.

M_ _ _

LOOk up

John chapter 20, verse 16 to see what the man said. Then fill in the letters.

As he spoke her name, Mary realised that this wasn't the gardener. It was Jesus and he was alive! She was so happy that she ran back to tell the good news to all the other friends of Jesus.

Can you find these words from the story in the wordsearch?

stone
angels
Mary
gardener
Jesus

a	x	M	i	j	p	l	r
n	o	a	x	y	e	J	o
g	a	r	d	e	n	e	r
e	s	y	z	t	f	s	x
l	r	p	l	z	b	u	c
s	t	o	n	e	d	s	e

Extra!

Make **Easter cards** for your family and friends. For each card, you will need an A4 piece of white card or stiff paper.

Fold the card in half. On the front, write **Happy Easter** in large letters.
Draw the tomb as shown, with a large stone shape in the middle.

Cut carefully along the dotted line. Do not cut the solid line.

On the inside, draw the angels as shown. Make sure that you can see the angels' faces and the words through the hole.
Use coloured pencils or crayons to decorate the card.
Whoever pulls back the stone will have a wonderful surprise (just like Mary did)!

You could make some **Easter biscuits** for tea. Ask a grown-up to help you.

You will need
350g (12oz) self-raising flour
1 teaspoon mixed spice
1 teaspoon cinnamon
175g (6oz) hard margarine
175g (6oz) sugar
110g (4oz) currants
2 beaten eggs

Method
1 Preheat the oven to 180° C, 350° F, gas mark 4.

2 Put the flour and spices into a bowl and rub in the margarine until the mixture looks like bread crumbs.

3 Stir in the sugar and currants.

4 Add the beaten eggs and knead until the dough is smooth.

5 On a floured surface, roll out to a thickness of ½ cm, then cut into rounds using a cutter.

6 Place on a baking sheet and bake for 15–20 minutes until golden brown.

Happy times

In the evening of the first Easter Sunday, two of Jesus' friends were walking home to their village a few miles away from Jerusalem. They had seen Jesus die on the cross and were feeling very sad. They were talking about what had happened. Suddenly a man joined them and started walking with them.

LOOk up
Luke chapter 24, verse 15 to find out who it was.

Write his name here: _ _ _ _ _

prayer time

Draw Jesus with the two friends.
They didn't recognise him.

These friends were very sad and puzzled, but Jesus walked next to them. Close your eyes and imagine Jesus sitting next to you. You cannot see him, but he really is there. Talk to him as you would to your family or friends.

Happy times

Jesus was walking with two friends who didn't recognise him. He noticed they were looking sad, so he asked them what they were talking about. They explained what had happened to their friend Jesus. They had heard about the empty tomb, but couldn't understand how Jesus could be alive.

Read **Luke chapter 24, verses 25 to 27** to see what Jesus said.

Jesus explained that long ago the prophets had said he would die and come alive again. He helped the friends to understand what had happened. When Jesus explained, the puzzle became clear. (But they still didn't recognise him!) Colour in the letters with a dot to make this puzzle become clear.

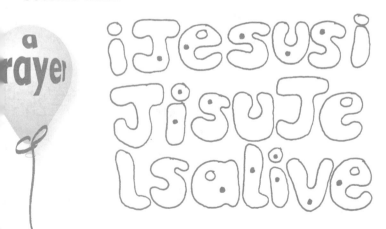

a prayer

Jesus, I don't always understand what is in the Bible. Help me to understand the most important things – that you are alive, that you love me and will never leave me.

Happy times

The two friends were walking with Jesus, but they didn't recognise him. At last they reached their house. It was getting dark, so they invited Jesus to stay the night with them. They sat down to have their supper.

LOOk up
Luke chapter 24, verses 30 to 31
to find out what Jesus did.

Which word goes where?

> blessed   broke   bread
>
> He _ _ _ _ _ _ _ the _ _ _ _ _. He _ _ _ _ _
> it and gave it to them.

At once the two friends knew who he was. (You read about the last time Jesus had broken bread on Day 11). Jesus disappeared, but they didn't mind. They knew that Jesus really was alive. They were so excited, they ran all the way back to Jerusalem to tell their friends that they had seen Jesus.

It's very dark now. Can you help them find their way?

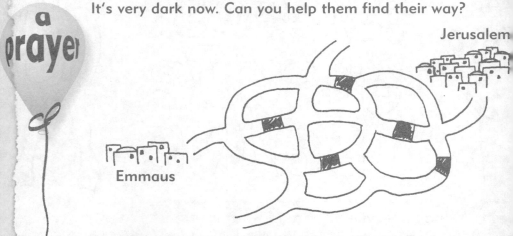

Jerusalem

a prayer

Emmaus

Dear Jesus, it's so great that you are really alive. Help me to share the good news with my friends.

Happy times

In Jerusalem, the friends of Jesus were talking together about Jesus coming back to life. Could it be true? Was Jesus really alive? Suddenly Jesus was in the room with them! They were terrified because they thought he was a ghost.

 Luke chapter 24, verses 38 to 39. What two things did Jesus tell them to do?

o k o l   o c u t h

_ _ _ _   _ _ _ _ _

Draw the marks on his hands where he had been nailed to the cross. They still weren't sure it was Jesus.

 verses 42 to 43 to see what they gave him. Draw it on the plate. (Ghosts don't eat fish!)

At last they knew that Jesus really was alive again.

prayer time

Jesus wants us to be sure that he is alive.
Say this prayer:
Thank you, Jesus, for the people who help me to understand that you really are alive.

Happy times

The friends told Thomas that they had seen Jesus alive again.

John chapter 20, verse 25.

What did Thomas say when he found out what he had missed? Colour in the word which fills the space in the sentence.

I do not

Know
See
Believe
Hear

a prayer

How do you feel if you miss out on something exciting? Draw your face here.

Dear God, sometimes I feel sad when I miss out on something exciting. Help me to know that you are there and understand how I feel.

Happy times

Jesus' friends were together again, but this time Thomas was with them. Join the dots to find out who joined them.

When Thomas saw Jesus, his doubts disappeared and he believed. What did Thomas and Jesus say to each other?

John chapter 20, verses 28 and 29 to find out. Thomas was so happy when he saw that Jesus was alive.

Say this prayer putting a word instead of the picture.
Dear God, knowing that you are near to me makes me feel like…

What else does knowing God is near make you feel like? Draw the pictures in the boxes.

Say the prayer again using each of your new words.

Happy times

Jesus' friends were together beside the lake.

What did Simon Peter say?

 John chapter 21, verse 3. Write it here.

What did the other friends say?

 a prayer

They fished all night. What did they catch? Read **John chapter 21, verse 3** again. Draw the empty fishing net.

Dear God, it's good to have friends. Thank you for my friends and the things we do together. Amen.

Happy times

Hello, I'm John. Do you remember when I went fishing with my friends? We fished all night and didn't catch anything. A man was standing on the beach. He shouted "What have you caught?" "Nothing," we shouted back. The man told us to try fishing on the other side of our boat.

Read John chapter 21, verse 6 and draw in what happened next.

Everyone was amazed at the number of fish in the net. Suddenly someone recognised the man. "It's Jesus," he shouted. Peter was so excited, he jumped into the water and swam to meet Jesus. The others followed in the boat. How do you think they felt as they sailed towards Jesus? Draw their faces.

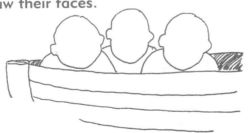

a prayer

Dear God, thank you that you know all about me. Thank you that you always know how I am feeling.

Happy times

It's John again.
Do you remember the day we caught a lot of fish? Who was waiting for us as we tried to land our catch? When we got to the shore, we found that Jesus had made a small fire. He had some food there, bread and fish. Peter pulled the catch ashore.

Read **John chapter 21, verses 9 to 11.** How many fish had they caught? Circle the right number.   **50   153   21**

They all sat down on the beach, and Jesus gave them bread and fish. What a breakfast that must have been! Can you spot five differences between these two pictures?

How happy the friends must have been to share breakfast with Jesus! Talk to God about times when you are happy. Draw or write your prayer in the fish shape.

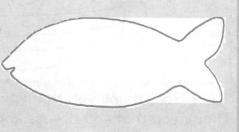

Extra!

A fishy sandwich to make
Talk about the story of the breakfast on the beach as you share a fishy sandwich with your friends or family.

You will need
an adult to help you, 2 slices of bread and a plate for each person, butter, fish paste, lettuce, cress, cucumber, spreading knives and a fish-shaped cutter.

1 Before you begin, wash your hands!
2 Spread the bread with butter and then with fish paste. Put one slice of bread on top of the other to make a sandwich.

3 Use the cutter to cut out a fish shape from the sandwich.
4 Wash the lettuce, cucumber and cress. Arrange the food as shown in the picture.
5 Make as many fishy sandwiches as you need.
6 Say "thank you" to God before enjoying your sandwiches together.

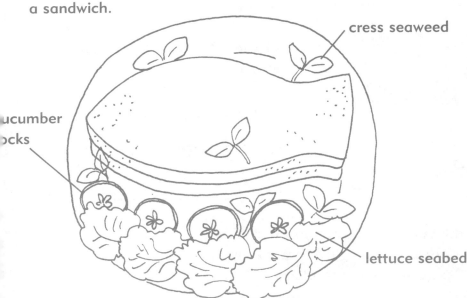

cress seaweed

ucumber
ocks

lettuce seabed

Amazing times

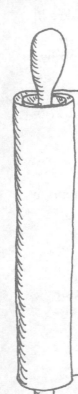

Peter's diary

What an amazing day! We were with Jesus on a mountain in Galilee where we first met him. He told us that it was time for him to go back to be with his Father God. We were surprised and a little afraid of being without him. But then he said, "You've got a lot of work to do, teaching people about me. Don't worry. You won't be able to see me, but I will be with you." Now that's wonderful – to have Jesus with us all the time!

Jesus promised to be with us, his friends.

Read **Matthew chapter 28, verse 20** to find out how long he'll be with us.

Put the words in the right order.

will   with   be   always   you   I

Jesus said, "__ ____ ____ ____

____ ____"

Thank you, Jesus, that you are with me right now. I'm glad that you will never leave me alone.

Extra!

Make this decoration to hang up and remind you that Jesus is with you.

You will need
a blank piece of card
glue
some felt tips or crayons
a hole-punch
some wool or string

Write on the card, or ask a grown up to write, in big letters: **Jesus is with me now.**

Colour the letters and decorate the card with patterns, flowers, animals or anything else you like. Or you could draw all the places you go to – school, swimming pool, church – to remind yourself that wherever you go, Jesus is with you.

Punch holes at the top near the middle. Thread your wool or string through the holes and tie the ends together.

Hang your decoration up. Look at it every day!

Amazing times

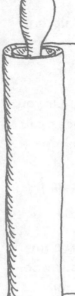

Peter's diary

Before Jesus went back to heaven, he told us (his friends) about the important work he wants us to do. He said we would be witnesses. That means we saw all the things that Jesus did and we heard all that he said, so we will be able to tell other people about him. Wow! Jesus has sent us to tell everyone about him!

Find out who Jesus was going to send to help his friends be witnesses. Read **Acts chapter 1, verse 8.**

Peter and his friends knew lots of stories about Jesus. Can you think of one that you know? If you are stuck, look at these pictures and tell someone what is happening.

Luke chapter 2, verses 5 to 7

Mark chapter 4, verses 35 to 41

Mark chapter 14, verses 22 to 23

Help me, Jesus, to listen to stories about you so that I will be able to tell others all the wonderful things you said and did.

Amazing times

Peter's diary
Do you remember that my friends and
I were talking with Jesus on a
mountain? As we were watching,
Jesus went up into heaven! A large
cloud came around him and we
couldn't see him any more. My friends
and I were still looking up at the sky.
Suddenly, we saw two men in white. I
think they were angels. They told us
something wonderful about Jesus.

What did the angels say?

Read **Acts chapter 1, verse 11,** then
colour the box which shows the
promise that Jesus' friends heard.
Cross out the wrong ones.

a prayer

| You will never see Jesus again | Jesus will come back again |

We don't know quite where,
And we don't know quite when,
But thank you, Lord Jesus,
That you'll come back again.

Jesus sends his love

Amazing times

Peter's diary

It's not usually much fun waiting for something, but we are waiting for the Holy Spirit and that's amazing! Jesus promised us that his helper, the Holy Spirit, would come soon. So all those who love Jesus – men, women, girls and boys – keep meeting together to pray. We don't know when the Holy Spirit will come. We don't know how it will happen. But we do know that it will be like getting a wonderful present. Jesus will only send something good. Our next meeting is on the special day we call Pentecost. I can't wait to see what will happen!

Some of these people were waiting with Peter for the Holy Spirit to come. Read **Acts chapter 1, verses 12 to 14** and put a tick next to their names. Cross out the ones who were not friends of Jesus.

prayer time

John ☐   Thomas ☐   King Herod ☐   Mary, Jesus' mother ☐   Pilate ☐

Thank Jesus for the good things he gives us, especially the Holy Spirit who helps us.

Amazing times

Peter's diary

It's amazing! The most wonderful thing that ever happened to me! The Holy Spirit has come and I'm filled with happiness! We were all meeting together at Pentecost. Suddenly we heard and saw things that told us the Holy Spirit had been sent from heaven. We all began to praise God at the top of our voices! I can't write much, I'm too busy dancing and singing for joy.

Do you know what Peter and the others heard and saw? Read **Acts chapter 2, verses 2 and 3** to find out. Then finish Peter's diary for him:

We heard a sound like a strong _ _ _ _ _ blowing.

i d n w

We saw what looked like tongues of _ _ _ _ _ .

i r e f

prayer time

Think of a joyful praise song that you could sing as you thank God for the Holy Spirit.

If you like, draw more flames over this page to remind you that the Holy Spirit is our helper now.

Amazing times

Peter's diary

On the day the Holy Spirit came, everything was so amazing! Just like Jesus had said, I was his witness! We were so full of joy that we couldn't stay indoors. We went outside, still praising God, and saw crowds of people there. And I began to tell them about Jesus! The Holy Spirit really helped me find the right words. I wasn't scared at all. I wonder if Jesus will want me to be a witness again. If he does, I know the Holy Spirit will help me.

LOOk up this story in **Acts chapter 2, verses 5 to 7.** Then find out how the crowd felt when they heard Jesus' friends praising God. Were they: **bored?** **angry?** **excited?**

Write the correct answer downwards in this crossword. Then put in the other words.

Clues

1 Who told the people about Jesus?

2 What special day was it? (See Day 34.)

3 Peter and the others received the Holy _____

4 Who is always with us? (See Day 30.)

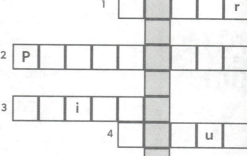

Dear Jesus, thank you for the amazing things that happen when we are your friends. Please help people who don't know you yet to hear about you and learn to love you.

The joke and puzzle page

Humpty Dumpty sat on
the wall
Quite out of reach of
anyone tall.
It's Easter egg time, so
he tucked up his feet
So he couldn't end up as
somebody's treat.

Knock knock.
Who's there?
Boy.
Boy who?
Boiled eggs for
breakfast, anyone?

You have learnt some exciting things about Jesus in
this book. Colour all the triangle shaped flags to
remind yourself of what they are.

a w H a k m e e d d i h d s m i o p l b e a e d x

H w e d c l a g m u e a p l i l v e k a g a o i n

H k e s d e n n t i t h p e l H o m l y f S a p i o r i f t

n b H r e w o y i l w l c o x m e b t b w a m c k l j

Look out for other **Join in – Jump on!** books.

Like reading stories? Look out for these exciting **Roller-coasters** and **Read by Myself** books!

If you feel you're ready to move on from **Join in – Jump on!**, try **Snapshots**. It's great!

All available from Scripture Union.

For more information ring 01908 856182 or contact your national office.